Word and Vision

original art and poetry

Sultan Khilji

Syncronis Publishing

Portland, Oregon

PUBLISHED BY

Syncronis Publishing
5331 SW Macadam Avenue, Suite 258-108
Portland, OR 97239

However, the author has chosen special paper for this book to allow for the careful removal and hanging of his art from your personal copy, should you elect to do so.

Word and Vision
By Sultan Khilji
ISBN 978-0-9706658-1-2
Poetry / Art

Book Design: Syncronis Publishing
Editor: Jeff Cantin
Art Direction: Debra Barnett
Cover Photograph: Self Portrait, Sultan Khilji
Cover and Interior Graphics: Jeff Cantin

Special thanks to Steve and the Team at Regal, Monica Do Coutto Monni, Rose Marie Raccioppi, Therese Lepage LaChapelle-Bhatnagar, Dagogo C. Wokoma, and Dr. Dheena Sadik…for taking time out of their busy schedules to review this book.

DEDICATED TO THE ONE WHO REMAINS

UNHEARD, UNSEEN AND UN-NAMED

Untitled (Oil on Canvas)

PROLOGUE

I love to read. I always have. While most children were reading comic books and detective stories I enmeshed myself in my Chinese reader, mythology's underground and tales from my favorite book—my father's big black tome of Edgar Allen Poe. Prep school and college years were filled with painting, poetry and the literary arts. How I wished I lived on the Left Bank in the time of Stein and the Last Generation. Ultimately lucky for me, though, as I have zero writing skills!

Fast forward to our Information Age and Facebook. Yes, Facebook … for this is where I first met Sultan Khilji. In my first few days of facebooking, I noticed that replying to friends' words gave access to all of *their* friends as well … and so it began. Why not create my own Paris and fill it with wonderful artists, musicians, poets and writers?

As I read my initial Khilji poems I *marveled*—"I am reading a modern day T.S. Eliot." And I wondered if he—as is customary in the Japanese culture—was a National Treasure of *his* country. Not wanting to appear ignorant, I asked him if he was published. Now, a few years and many great conversations later, I am so happy to share with you not only his poetry—but also a glimpse into this extraordinary man via his art. Enjoy!

—Debra Barnett, CEO
Syncronis Publishing

Table of Contents

Who Am I?

Who am I, but a question hidden in an answer.
Who am I, but a leaf that spring forgot to bear.
Who am I, but a mute echo lost in a scream.
Who am I, but black veiled in white.
Who am I, but a tear concealed in a calculated smile.

Who am I…

I am the answer, if you are willing to ask.
I am spring, if you promise never to forget.
I am the voice, if you understand the silence.
I am all the colors, if you wish to see the rainbow.
I am true happiness, if you vow to never break a heart.

I am, if you are.

I am, YOU, and not you.

The Sunflower (Oil on Canvas)

ACHTUNG

Beware!
This is not poetry
No words
Pearls strung in rhyme
or reason
Beautiful flowers, love
Instant Clichéd wisdom
An effervescent pill
Orange flavored
bubbling away in chilled water
This is not a painting either
Brushstrokes of Muso Soseki
Laden with paint
Thick, dripping emotion:

"別 無 工 夫"

This is expression
of another kind
This is the no-sound
Can you hear me?

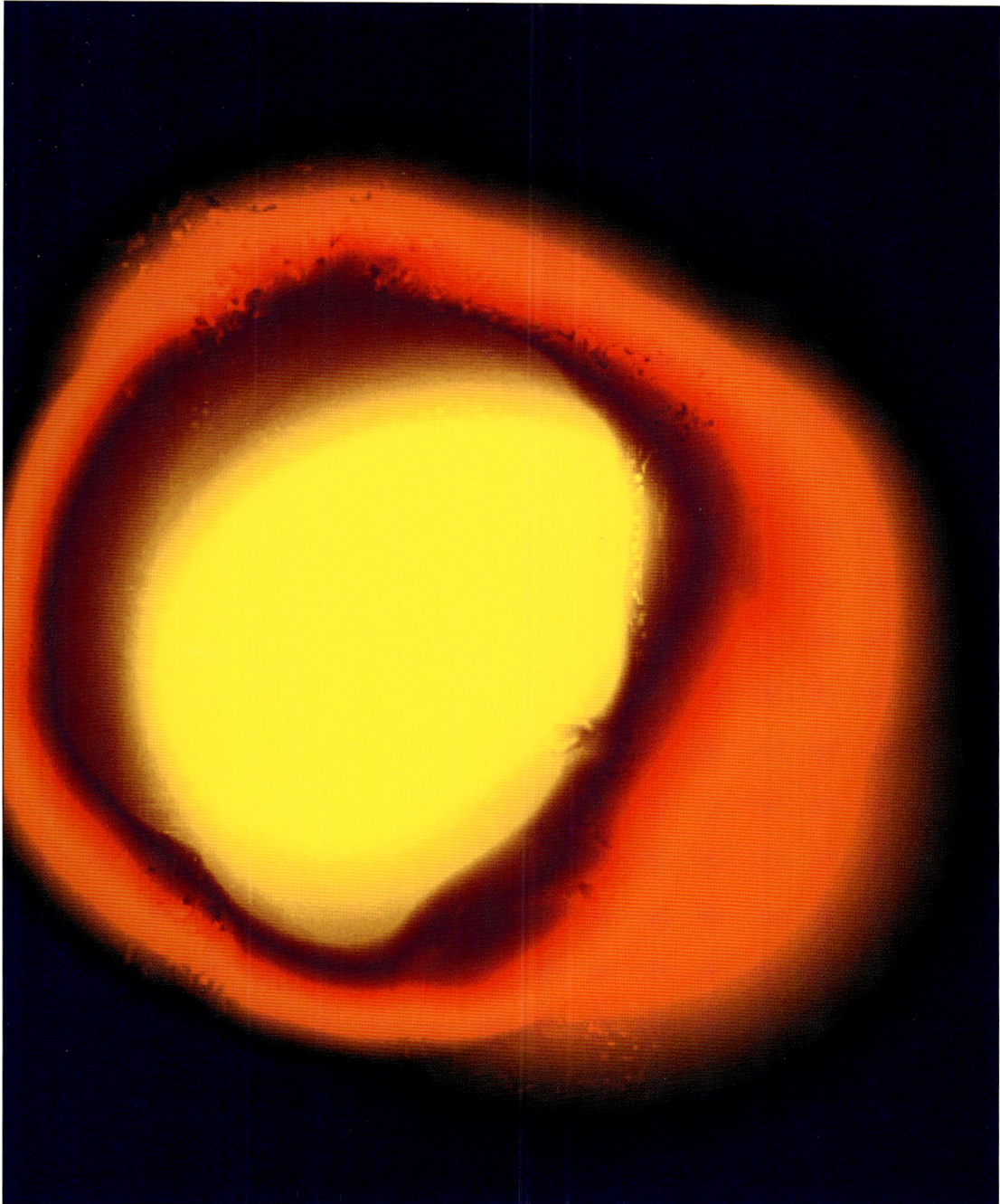

Creation—Self Portrait (Watercolor on Photographic Paper, Digitally Altered)

THE DANCE

The night grows cold.
Whisper the shadows,
passing through the crowds,
of a myriad souls…

Wandering aimlessly in the fog of dread;
Dancing, like a bird without a head.

The shrieking trumpets of silence blow;
Dancing…
We sway in the arms,
that never show.

Dance (Oil on Canvas)

BEHIND THIS DOOR

Behind this door
That never did open
Lay my tended garden,
No one ever did explore.

Sunflowers, daisies, and roses,
All colors kept alive & bright
By the springs that flow,
With waters sweet, reflecting light.

Many came; some returned,
Thinking it was locked;
Some stayed and looked around,
Yet never found a key.

Funny how they now complain
When they could've knocked,
Or just asked me?

The Pagoda (Oil and Acrylic on Paper)

THE BEING IN NON-BEING

The Sun, The Moon, And Song
Were made by the Beloved,
and The Beloved, made for me.
But all lost meaning, like trinkets…
Self, verse, rose, flute
The stars, and sky…
When Love's Lyre plucked its chord,
Heaven's Light was I.

Magic Sun (Watercolor on Cold-Pressed Paper, Laquered)

Autumn

'I was alive once…and that was when you were not dead.'

The voice echoed through the thunderous rain and I never even noticed for once, the other coffin that lay beside yours. Maybe it wasn't even there till they offered you to the black soil on that bleak September night. Maybe I was too engrossed in myself to notice, or maybe I was too wrapped up in you to feel life drain out of me into that abysmal hole in the ground that only seemed six feet deep at that time. Even they never noticed. But then, how could they anyway? The blind are never supposed to see. Or are they?

Maybe they chose not to see…or maybe their demons curtained it from their view by sheer force of evil. They think they are their companions for eternity, but they are not. They'll live with their demons till they die…but they'll die alone. His or her demon will move on to someone else, perhaps to her or perhaps to him, again, to haunt him or her to eternity.

As for me, I'll just lie here…alone. With no angel or demon to keep me company. For I am one who has found permanent companionship with solitude itself. I have seen the light in the supreme darkness of its nothingness. I have heard the whispers of solace echoing through its silent vales. I have found love and sympathy cradled in the tentacles of scorn within it…I have found my voice, but have lost the words.

But I know. I'll live within this death till it dies. And they will learn to let their demons go, and awaken with their hearts not blind anymore. They will see that other coffin…lay it beside yours and cover it with the black soil of that bleak September night. And a voice shall echo through the cemetery…

'I was dead once…that was when you were not alive, but now I am alive within your death.'

The Trees (Watercolor and Ink on Cold-Pressed Paper)

This Fire

Words won't kill
This hunger
That lingers.

No sun will calm
These shivers
Down the spine.

This Fire
That burns
With water
That creeps
Down the brow

Will die

Only With Fire…

Creation-Fire (Watercolor on Photograph, Digitally Altered)

Amaryllis (Bitter Honey)

Scarlet.
Blood of white
in veins turning green;
Wither it shall in the end,
but life shall ever be
Reincarnated,
like a phoenix from the flames.

The seeds of wrath sown,
bloom yet of gore…

Forevermore.

The bitter fruit of love,
ever sweeter than this honey,
from the flowers of gloom that grow
in the bosom of this child of woe.

This tended thorn
of loving scorn
shall stay…

Forevermore.

Amaryllis (Watercolor on Paper)

A Prayer

"Humbled,
come I into this Sanctuary.

With Love and Faith,
From those who have gone before.

Innocent am I in understanding,
Holy and pure in my love,
of all that is good and blessed.

Supreme God,
Ruler of The Light,
Lord of all!
Hear my prayer,
Help me now to dispel
All negativity,
All shadows of darkness
That doom themselves
to shame and unhappiness.

Save them;
Make them part of the Light.

Mercy is Thy song I sing;
Forgiveness the act most precious.

In Thy Everlasting Grace,
I say this.
In humility,
I ask this.

Amen."

Jesus (Watercolor and Ink on Cold-Pressed Paper)

Mother

Come meet me today, Dear Mother,
I lie in wait for that softest Love;
of your precious hands, none other,
Wrinkled, by the timeless wind above.

Gather me up, these forgotten withered petals are I,
Soak life unto this grave's soil with tears you cry;
Come, Take me back in to your loving embrace,
I'm lost as an echo in this void with a hollow face.

Then in to this haunting wind, sprinkle me,
Like the fragrance, of a thousand blooms;
That lives a long spring, not fade too soon,
Carried away, and blurred in to a memory...

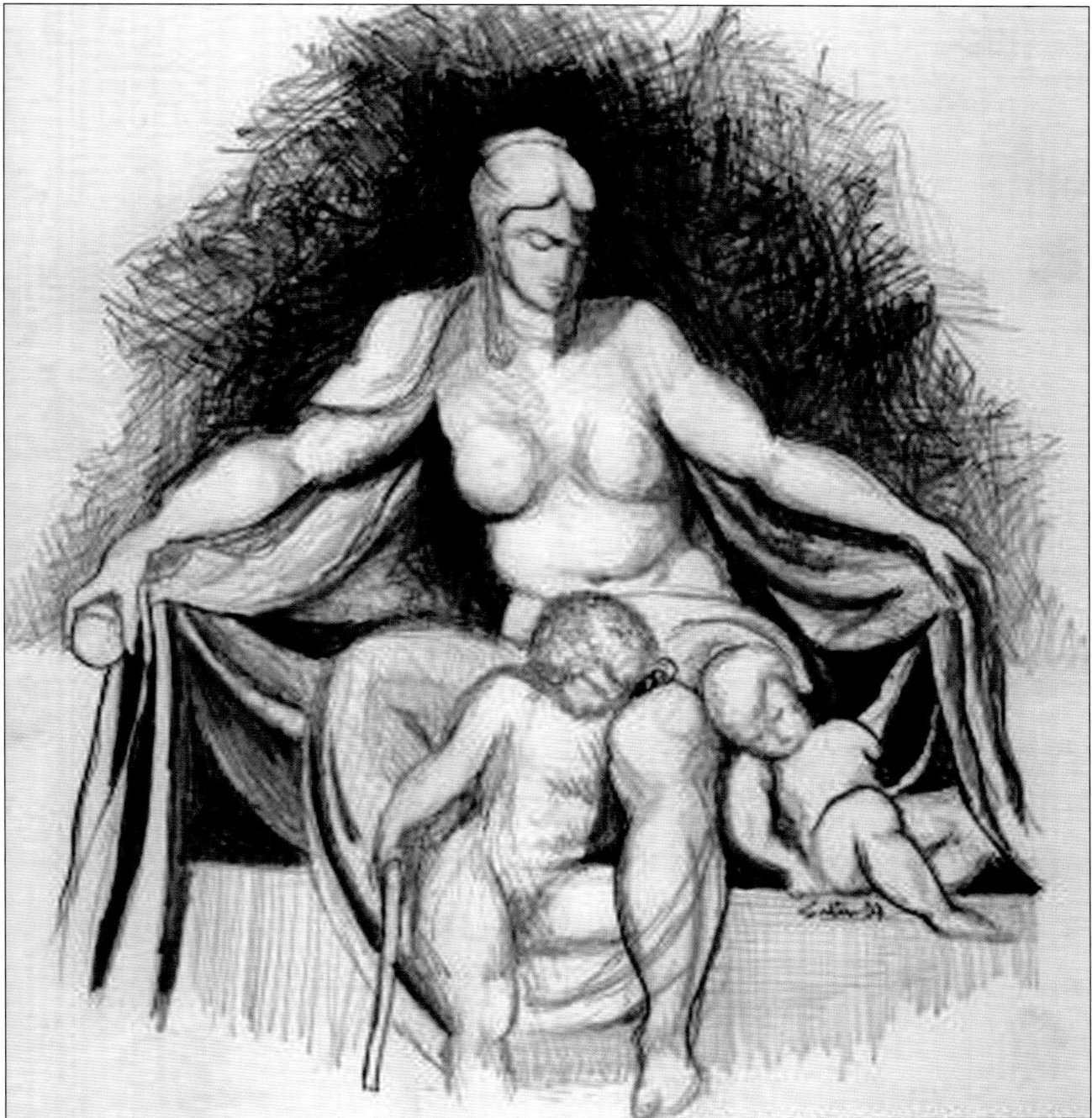

Night with Her Children Sleep and Death (Graphite on Paper)

HAPPINESS

Every morning you wake up to the clock;
You promise yourself you will find it today,
Just like you tried yesterday.
You sweep all your misery under the rug; it's quite a chore.
You put on your coat and glasses, as you step out the door.
You look for it 'round every corner,
Every alley, every street;
You seek it in every stranger,
Every friend that you greet.
You buy a paper, a coffee from the road-side café;
"There's not a sign of it anywhere," to yourself, I hear you say.
You take the bus and lose yourself in the rush of the day.
Work? No, it can't be here! Not ever, in this monotonous
    affair!
You take the bus back, finish your crossword on the way.
"What's that nine-letter word?" I hear you say
To every passenger, and not to yourself this time.
"We are sorry, but we don't know!"
Funny, you think... the same answer, every time!
You fold the paper and put it in your bag;
You look out the window and wonder
How the day's been such a drag!
You hope that night would be different,
As you let out a sigh and of course, a prayer.
You hit a club before going home;
SO many people, you are sure
Someone will have enough to share.
You walk through the crowds,
You dance, you buy someone a drink;
A kind gesture will surely get you some,
Hah! You Think!
"Not tonight, not here," says the bartender
as you tell him for what you ask;

"These smiles are all hollow; these people, they wear a mask."
"What a waste, haven't found it even today," I hear you say.
You leave as empty as you entered.
You walk back to your house, Kicking a can along the way.
You unlock the door and you enter;
You stumble on the same misery
You'd so conveniently swept under.
You take off your coat and hang it on the stand.
Rain starts to fall as you straighten out the rug.
You take a book off the shelf and cozy up under the blanket.
Loud mixed with muffled, rolls the thunder,
"How to find Happiness," it says in bold on the cover.
Rain pounds wildly on the window pane,
As you flip through the pages,
But of course, in vain!
Your head starts to ache, and soon it does spin,
You get out of bed, and dunk the book in the bin.
You return to bed, set the clock for the same time
As always, as you swallow some mild aspirin
And you try to sleep despite the storm's ongoing din.
You finally drift off to sleep after a many toss, turn and curl,
And as you drift off, from your palm drops down a glittering
    pearl.
It rolls itself down the bed in a quiet, hastened hurl
To join a few thousand of its own clan.
Glowing all so bright,
Each one from every past night
Says the new to the others as you dream another plan,
"He's missed me again, this Poor Man!
Won't it be just grand...
If only he'd stop searching around
And look for me...
In his own hand!?!"

Dreams (Acrylic on Paper, Lacquered)

THE MUTE NIGHTINGALE

Upon the barren branch, the mute nightingale sits,
The Rose it cannot see, hence no song warm and tender;
Behind the autumn veils, many a bud forever waits,
For melody borne on air, to unfurl its hidden splendor . . .

Days Work Done (Watercolor on Paper)

THE UNSAID

Let's sit together for hours.
Let's communicate in silence.
Let's drain our hearts
of all this pain,
Without the quivering of a lip.
Let's not think.
Let's be blind and numb too
To all there is that's left,
The Unsaid.

Let's then part smiling,
Pretend we understand each other.
Let's wait in silence
Till we meet again;
Next weekend, perhaps?
Let's sit together a while,
Say all there is
Till there's nothing left,
All Things said.

And go our separate ways,
Never to meet again!

The Unsaid—Self Portrait (Photograph, Digitally Altered)

Time [18]

"Time shall heal"
All here or not,
All hurt or not;
"It shall endure"
Till it doesn't?
"Time shall teach,"
Yet never yield?
Till you are,
or not.

And then some more,
Of Time.

"It shall remind"
Over and over,
In vicious cycles
Like the hands of a clock,
This all Sadistic One,
That soothes
Every jab
Of its Three-edged-sword!
By sugarcoating it
As "experience?"

Give it 18
And reap the one still green?
Give it all
And reap the one barely gold?

Oh ye, Great Deceiving One!
Know,
"The sweetest fruit lay
With what has an End…"

Does thee?
Before Me?

Creation-Time (Oil Pastels on Paper)

THE TRAVELER

Dawn breaks, and he walks
Through a desert that never ends.
To his heart alone, he talks
Upon the dunes' twists and bends.

Tumbleweeds, the racing companions,
He rolls along the howling wind;
Pass by many forgotten tombstones,
and vows he never to give in.

The heat, it scorches his skin;
the glare, it dazzles his eyes.
The sand in the air blinds him,
and beneath his feet, it fries.

Bogged down by thirst for water,
By dusk, courage begins to wane.
He falls against a cactus's shelter,
Body numb to the prickles of pain.

When all seems lost and gone,
Barely Hopeful, he closes his eye.
Clouds appear on the horizon,
In the desert forever dry.

Percussions of tiny raindrops
and the thunder's drum begin;
The skies glow with lightening,
And the breeze begins to sing.

Fear dissolves and out it steeps,
He curls up in peace and sleeps
Till the break of the dawn's hue.
Parched lips drenched anew,
His Soul lights up and smiles,
and he walks for miles and miles.

For every bliss that's earned
In this cycle of Night and Day,
and for every wisdom learned,
Here is what I have to say:

Not all days are warm and sunny,
Not all nights are cold and drear;
So whatever Life may bring thee,
With Faith, O Traveler, persevere!

The Desert (Oil and Oil Pastels on Canvas)

PERSONAL FEELINGS

Keep them buried,
Where they belong,
Deep within,
Far from every wrong.

Don't make public,
What is personal!
Unless…
you want to fit
A square bit
In the round puzzle
Of their limited wit.

A blazing fuel to their egos,
A bitter poison for you,
There's no doubt;
These personal feelings
Fare better in, than out.

Why not to yourself be kind?
Can you afford to be misread
One more time?

The Water Tower (Oil on Cardboard)

THE STORY

The child stood in the doorway, a silhouette against the bright light in the background. "Do you remember me?" whispered the child. As I tried to part my lips to speak, he said, "say no more."

I turned around to the others. They all wore masks of blue. I took one from the table and put it on my face. The door was closed, the child gone.

"Would you like some tea?" "I would surely love some." I said to my companion sitting across the table. We indulged in the ritual, silently pouring the brew, mixing the various ingredients presented in intricately patterned china. Faint smiles exchanged as the cup was presented to me.

A slight pause of silence was the cue that something had to be spoken but I lowered my gaze in to the cup and started to stir the tea, elegantly as I could, trying to dissolve the sugar that had already been diffused before the cup was given to me. Clearly I had nothing to say. Or perhaps I did but I did not want to let out the words pacing impatiently on my tongue. I took a sip and swallowed them back in to my stomach.

I looked back at the door. It was still closed. "Is everything alright? Are you getting late?" My companion asked. "Yes, everything is just fine. I need to leave, it is late." Said I, as I excused myself from the table and left the room.

The streets were bare as I walked back home. A faint flash of lightening and distant rumble of the clouds announced rains coming, or was it a remnant note of last night's storm? I asked myself as I started counting, "One one thousand, Two one thousand, Three one thousand…" waiting for the next flash and rumble, to gauge whether the clouds were

receding or approaching, but it never happened. I stopped counting and continued to walk. Long paces gradually turned smaller, and I reached home.

"Dinner's in the oven!" I heard my mother. "I'm not hungry. I had something to eat earlier." I hung my coat on the rack and went upstairs to my room. I changed and tucked myself in to bed. And just then I realized I still had the mask on! It took quite a struggle taking it off. It was as if it had somehow diffused with my skin. Eventually, it did come off, and I was relieved. "That was so silly! I am just glad no one saw me on the street, 'specially mum!" It didn't take too long before I was fast asleep.

I ran past the mountains, deserts, and swam through the seas while it rained and snowed with bright sunlight all at the same time, till I finally fell down in a vast green field and disappeared.

"Wake up! It's nine! You don't want to be late now, do you?" I heard my mother. I got up, changed, had breakfast, and left the house as always. Took the same bus and arrived at the same place.

I stood at the door. Inside the room the lights were dim compared to the bright sunlit day outside. My eyes searched for him and then I was finally able to find him standing next to a large table, still a bit away from the crowd. He turned and looked at me.

"Do you remember me?" I asked. And as he parted his lips to speak, I said, "Say no more." And left.

Man (Oil Pastels on Paper, Lacquered)

DEPENDENCE

Strolled out of this shell,
A night or three, two years ago;
Stumbled a few steps and fell,
No further could I go.

This sweet poisoned drink
To these parched lips, you pressed.
Stung, paralyzed, I couldn't think,
And although my eyes were open,
True world disappeared, seemed dead.

I merrily lived visions
Of your hallucinations;
Fed generously to my head,
Wove so gently, through this skin,
You strung my limbs on a thread.

You pulled me here
and pushed me there,
I never felt so free.
In your manipulating hands,
A mute puppet, I let myself be,
Yet strangely, felt so happy.

Your drug I craved, that sweet poison,
And you, my sole provider,
Took my hand, when I flew higher.
You stole my own horizon.

Took all you wanted, and you let go,
I fell out of the sky.
No one heard, and no one saw;
The drug wore off,
and I…was I!

Dependence (Watercolor on Paper)

Tomorrow

Today she told me
about tomorrow
Or was it yesterday
I can't recall
"But while in sleep", she said,
"Always a hint of wake
and while awake, a subtle slumber.
Life rendered sweet
with a pinch of salt,
Death kept in melancholic surrender."
So, upon this star-laden floor I lie
And gaze in to a sky of velvet grass
studded with flowers
of galactic abundance
Fireflies swirl around me
in a ballet of golden stardust
And I remain,
about to awake
from a slumber
a divine metamorphosis
in to the only butterfly
in this magical realm...
Like A spell
that manifests itself
before it ever finds the words...

The House (Watercolor on Paper, Varnished)

Sailing

Go on… Go on…
Let the wind guide you
Through the turbulent waves…
Escape the lullabies
of the calm ocean,
The calls of the banshees,
The Sirens
that would enchant you
into the abyss of oblivion.
Go on…
Rip past the sands of the shore
through the rocky cliffs,
beyond the scorching, thirsting deserts.
Glide across the calm green pastures;
Heed not the call of intoxication,
The little white flowers,
The Venus Fly Traps.
Go on… Go on…
Pierce through the forests
to the foot of the mountain.

Let not the sheer majesty
of height
Dazzle and intimidate
into defeat.
The last trick of illusion
The wind in your sails…
it is truly enough
If you believe in its power.
Persist and conquer;
Leave the ground.
Soar… Soar…
Across the skies,
past the clouds, the rain,
and the Sun,
Into those unfurling Arms
that wait
for this ship's return home.
Dock well
and drop the anchor.

Going Fishing (Watercolor on Paper)

The Kimono

"Hold still!" She says sternly, as she ties the last of the layers of the kimono in place with an elegant knot. Mother, it feels as a serpent coiled tightly around its victim fiercely trying to squeeze the last breath out of me. Another yank on my shoulder and she spins me around, and I stand facing her. Her movements are perfect and calculated and it is no surprise to me. It is a ritual we go through every morning.

I look in to her eyes as I wait for her to pass the ivory comb through my hair next, traversing flawless straight lines without even a hint of a slight swerve.

I would love to run to the pond to feed the Koi right now but they never come to the surface these days, in the dead of winter. Nothing does. Everything sinks in to its depths or gets blanketed over by the snow. Even the water turns gray before freezing over. Layers upon layers piling up… like unknown unpaid debts of borrowed smiles gathered every day.

Today's different though. There are no debts to pay even though I wish to smile. The house is in mourning. Black is the color of the day. Only the blues and the red are missing. They will never visit us now. Last I saw them; they were clenched tightly in your fist just before they closed the lid on you. "You're the most beautiful thing ever happened to me." You once said. Yes, I am. I wish I could say the same to you, but there's no need to lie anymore.

The guests would arrive soon. Condolences and later, half-turned smiles, a pat on the head, a praising of the exquisite kimono.. I can almost hear you call me to the dining room.. The intricate aroma wafting from the kitchen fills the house.

If I could just run away right now.. But this huge ocean of neatly parked shoes outside the door is just too great a leap for these small feet to accomplish. So I'll stay and wait for the guests to leave, as I do, every day…

The Kimono (Acrylics on Laminated Board)

Thank You, Goodbye

Thank you

For the endless hours
Of senseless fun.

For being there
always,
When YOU craved company
When you had nothing better to do.

For your surprise calls
At your convenience.

For those "selfless" limits
To your sincerity.

For understanding me,
In your own way.

For your equality,
In calculated give and take.

For your undying support,
As long as I was afloat.
For your self-confessed inability
In saying "no" to me,
And the generous frequency
of saying "no!"
Thank you, most of all,
For the punch marks on the walls!

That bore the final Goodbye!

Anticipation (Dry Pastels on Paper, Varnished)

MAGIC SPACE NINE

Of a hundred years, veiled in mirrors amillion,
Silken pages, weaved therein, thoughts un-torn;
Threads of Gold streaming, in fabric vermilion,
Bound in pristine velvet covers, this story born.

Thrown in a cauldron, madly bubbling away,
Fed alive by Fire, lightning and thunder;
And upon it, clouds, in a spell-like sway,
Melancholy awake from her unknown slumber.

She stirred in storms and I, poured calm;
Ingredients all-thought and never-thought,
In a frenzied flood, rolling off each palm.
A battle of Love and chaos both I's fought.

Win Love did, as ever, in the end,
for even storm puts chaos to mend.
But that's not the point you see, as such is Love's fate;
The point therein I tell, is all that I did in the end create:

An existence Void of Fire, Water, Air, or Earth,
One with no smile, no tear, no death, no birth.
And then I, forever sealed this Riddle Divine,
Within this visible-invisible Magic Space Nine.

Of no tree, a strange and bitter fruit,
Bursting therein the sweetest of honey,
I remain, a Child of no blossom, no bee;
Imprisoned by limitless fields and skies.
From what do tell, is she to set me free?

And so now, kept at a distance, she stands
with a million keys with no locks to be seen;
Poor ol' Melancholy cries and rubs her hands,
Being the perfect her, and I, the perfect Me.

All said, and yet this Tale too long to untell,
All words I shall now banish off the ink.
Of all talk I am tired; I've fared it well,
For good, From My Magic Kingdom Within.

The Pond (Watercolor on Cold-Pressed Paper, Lacquered)

SPRING

The autumn leaves sigh
Withered expression,
hallowed gaze
Dreams crumble
Beneath each footstep
Weighed down
dried branches cry
Watching over me
through the dusty haze

Passing through this forest
of twisted labyrinthine paths
Strewn with painful revelations
Imprisoned
By Truth's despicable clutches
This Soul awaits redemption
that lay cradled within
The Lie of Spring...

Man in a Cabbage Field (Oil on Canvas, Pasted on Hardboard)

SECRETS

If I wished I can tell you today,
Secrets to a bright sunny day;
I can sing you the Song of Rain,
...to wash away all Winter's Gray.

Steal Spring's Rainbows, Summer's Gold
and all Autumn's whispers seldom told;
Cause the sun to sink and bring a certain moon,
moonless nights too, only banished too soon.

But I shall keep this all for tomorrow,
Let Secrets live till some never-day;
Leave this thorn be that causes pain,
That bleeds Life in to the Crimson Rose;
For without thorn, no Rose does remain.

So I shall leave this Soul to sing,
Clouds bring, and snows to fall;
for these bare feet to leave prints,
only to melt with the Sun's call.

In Spring (Oil on Canvas)

I

Upon Zephyr's wings in the morning sky,
A crystalline drop of dew descended I.
Enlivening barren lands, tiptoed barefoot,
Eyes' magic caused blooms, leaves and root.

Forever concealed, a secret, I,
Like butterflies playing hide and seek;
Rainbows painted across the sky,
As wings flutter colorful silken sleek.

Unbound by pristine walls, forts of mortal queen and king,
'Tis I to Nature's wild, playful children discipline bring;
My kisses of Life make buds to flowers, all birds to sing,
Awaking the sleepy acorn from which the mighty Oak Spring.

I Emerald grass, ruby roses and I forever Sapphire's streams,
Forever Sun-bright I shine, I sound sleep in moonlight beams.

Maiden with the Sunflowers (Watercolor and Ink on Paper)

Fell in love with an image?

Limited editions of Mr. Khilji's work have been hand printed onto elegant, archival cotton Rag. Visit Sultan Khilji's website to see more information about this beautiful series including image sizes, availability and price … .

www.magicspacenine.com

The wonderful thing about poetry is that you can enjoy it privately in a stolen moment; or you can share it with friends in a lively discussion at your Book Club.

Use the Book Club button at magicspacenine for special group rates when shipping all books to one address.

Teachers, professors and schools may also use this special rate.

Independent Bookstore Owners—if WORD and VISION is not currently available through your distributors we are happy to ship directly to your bookstore at standard industry prices.

Notes